# HOW THE WORLD MAKES MUSIC

# PIANOS AND KEYBOARDS

## ANITA GANERI

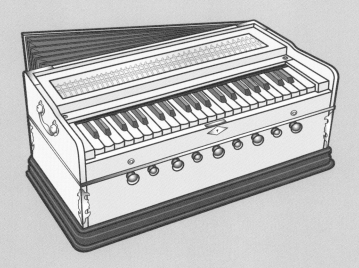

**W**
# FRANKLIN WATTS
LONDON • SYDNEY

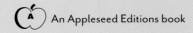 An Appleseed Editions book

First published in 2011 by Franklin Watts
338 Euston Road, London NW1 3BH

Franklin Watts Australia
Hachette Children's Books
Level 17/207 Kent St, Sydney, NSW 2000

© 2011 Appleseed Editions

Created by Appleseed Editions Ltd,
Well House, Friars Hill, Guestling,
East Sussex TN35 4ET

Designed by Guy Callaby
Illustrated by Graham Rosewarne
Edited by Jinny Johnson
Picture research by Su Alexander

ISBN 978-1-4451-0356-3

Dewey Classification: 786

A CIP catalogue for this book is available from the British Library.

Picture credits
l = left, r = right, t = top, b = bottom
Title page l Ray Evans/Alamy, cl 3355M/Shutterstock, cr Pep Roig/Alamy, r Lebrecht Music and
Arts Photo Library/Alamy; Contents page Stuart Dow/Shutterstock; P4 Lebrecht Music and Arts
Photo Library/Alamy; 5 Svemir/Shutterstock, Objectsforall/Shutterstock, Sbarabu/Shutterstock,
Lebrecht Music and Arts Photo Library/Alamy, Marco Bradic/Shutterstock; 7t Craig Lovell/Eagle
Visions Photography/Alamy, b Lebrecht Music and Arts Photo Library/Alamy; 8 Losevsky Pavel/
Shutterstock; 9 Ronald Caswell/Shutterstock; 10 The Art Gallery Collection/Alamy; 12 & 13
Lebrecht Music and Arts Photo Library; 14 Lebrecht Music and Arts Photo Library/Alamy;
15 Antonio Poves; 16 Lebrecht Music and Arts Photo Library/Alamy; 17 Stuart Dow/Shutterstock;
19 Danita Delimont/Alamy; 20 Amoret Tanner/Alamy; 21 Pep Roig/Alamy; 22 Ray Evans/Alamy;
24 Simon Price/Alamy; 25 Lebrecht Music and Arts Photo Library/Alamy; 26 Nikita Rogul/
Shutterstock; 28 3355M/Shutterstock; 29 Getty Images.

Front cover: main image Jupiterimages/Thinkstock; background image Viachaslav Kraskouski/
Shutterstock; top row (left to right) LionH/Shutterstock; Pavel/Shutterstock; 3355M/
Shutterstock; Karam Miri/Shutterstock

Printed in Singapore

Franklin Watts is a division of Hachette Children's Books,
an Hachette UK company.
www.hachette.co.uk

# Contents

Pianos and keyboards    4

Piano    6

Grand piano and pianola    8

Harpsichord    10

Clavichord    12

Hurdy gurdy    14

Church organ    16

Accordion    18

Harmonium    20

Melodica    22

Carillon and celeste    24

Electronic keyboard    26

Synthesizer    28

Words to remember    30

Index    32

# Pianos and keyboards

People all over the world make music. They play musical instruments and sing songs when they are happy or sad, and as part of festivals and other ceremonies. People enjoy listening to music as they go about their daily lives.

*A pianist playing in a concert, accompanied by an orchestra. Keyboards may also be played as solo instruments.*

## Musical keyboards

There are many different types of musical instruments. This book is about keyboard instruments, from pianos and organs, to accordions and electronic keyboards. These instruments make music in different ways (see box) but they are all played by pressing the keys on a keyboard. Keyboard instruments can be played alone, or accompanied by an orchestra. They are important in classical music, pop and jazz, and in religious and folk music around the world.

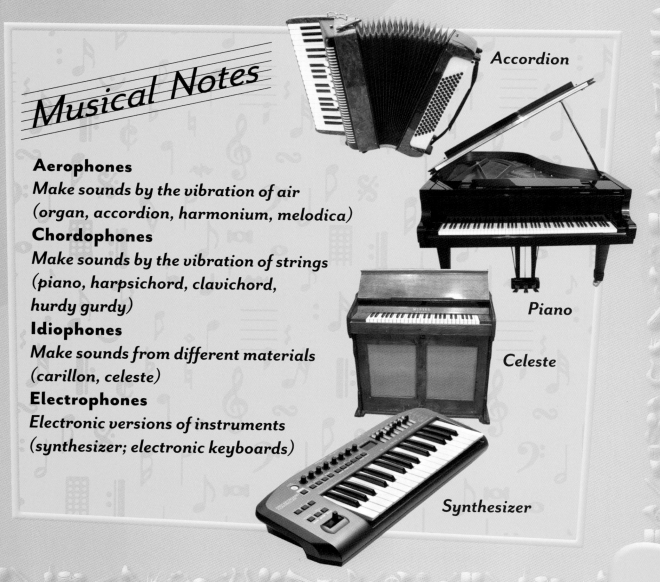

## Musical Notes

**Aerophones**
*Make sounds by the vibration of air (organ, accordion, harmonium, melodica)*
**Chordophones**
*Make sounds by the vibration of strings (piano, harpsichord, clavichord, hurdy gurdy)*
**Idiophones**
*Make sounds from different materials (carillon, celeste)*
**Electrophones**
*Electronic versions of instruments (synthesizer; electronic keyboards)*

Accordion

Piano

Celeste

Synthesizer

# Piano

The piano's full name is 'pianoforte' which means 'soft-loud' in Italian. Because they are so expressive, pianos are used to play a wide range of styles of music.

## Piano parts

Most pianos have a wooden case, with a metal frame inside, from which metal strings are stretched. The hammers, which strike the strings, are made from wood, covered in felt. The keyboard has 88 keys – 36 black keys and 52 white keys. In the past, the keys were made from ivory (white) and ebony (black) but, today, they are usually made from wood, covered in plastic.

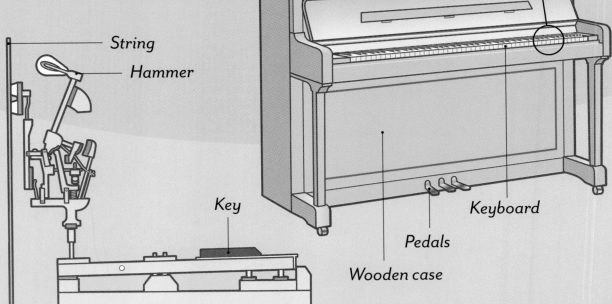

Black keys

White keys

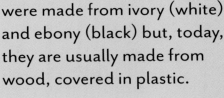

String

Hammer

Key

Keyboard

Pedals

Wooden case

## Piano playing

When the player presses a key, a hammer strikes a string and causes it to vibrate. The player can change the sound by pressing the keys hard or softly, and by pressing the pedals with his feet. A pianist must be able to read two lines of music at once, and play separate notes with each hand.

*It takes years of practice to become a good pianist and develop a good playing technique.*

## Musical Notes

The piano is thought to have been invented by Italian instrument-maker, Bartolomeu Cristofori (1655 – 1731). He worked for Prince Ferdinando de Medici, looking after his collection of musical instruments.

# Grand piano

A grand piano has the same parts as an upright piano but the frame and strings are arranged horizontally instead of vertically. The case is shaped to hold the long bass strings, curving in for the shorter treble strings. Full-sized grand pianos make a rich, warm sound and are often played in concerts.

*The piano lid can be opened to project the sound.*

## Grand sizes

There are many different sizes of grand piano. The three most important are:

● Baby grand (up to 1.7 metres long]

● Parlour grand (1.7–2.2 metres long)

● Concert grand (2.2–3 metres long)

# Pianola

Pianolas are automatic pianos which were popular in the early 20th century. Inside, there are rolls of paper, with perforations punched into them. Each perforation stands for a musical note. As the rolls turn, they pass over a cylinder pierced with holes. This causes the hammers to strike the piano strings.

*A pianola is like a piano with rolls of music inside.*

As the notes play, the keys on the keyboard press down. So, players can pretend to be playing a piece of music, even if they have never played a piano before. They can choose from classical, popular or religious music. Many pianists and composers have recorded music especially for the pianola.

# Harpsichord

**H**arpsichords were very popular instruments in the 17th and 18th centuries. People played them at home and in chamber music groups. They give a bright, clear and precise sound. Later, harpsichords fell out of favour as pianos became more popular. Today, electronic harpsichords are sometimes used to play rock and pop music.

*A harpsichord can have several keyboards, called manuals. This one dates from the 18th century.*

## Musical Notes

*King Henry VIII of England was a keen musician. Among his collection of musical instruments were 78 recorders, 78 flutes, five sets of bagpipes and a virginal (an instrument like a harpsichord but in a rectangular box).*

## Harpsichord shape

A harpsichord is wing- or harp-shaped, like a baby grand piano. The strings stretch horizontally away from the keyboard. The long, bass strings for the low notes are on the left; the shorter, treble strings for higher notes are on the right. Harpsichords have wooden cases, and are often beautifully decorated. Some stand on legs. Others are placed on a table, and are ususally played standing up.

## Harpsichord music

To play the harpsichord, a player presses a key on the keyboard. This lifts up a long strip of wood, called a jack. Attached to the jack is a plectrum, made of quill or plastic. The plectrum plucks a string to make a sound. There is a jack and plectrum for each key. A harpsichord may have one, two, or even three sets of keys, called manuals.

Bass strings

Treble strings

Keyboards
(manuals)

Wooden
case

Legs

# Clavichord

Like harpsichords, clavichords are stringed keyboard instruments. They date back to the 14th century but were most popular in Europe in the 16th and 17th centuries. But, because they could not make a loud sound, they were more suitable for playing at home.

## Musical Notes

A story tells how famous German composer, Georg Friedrich Handel, was not allowed to have musical instruments in his house. His father wanted him to study law, not music. But Handel smuggled a small clavichord into the attic and practised secretly at night.

*Some clavichords had beautifully decorated cases and lids.*

*This clavichord was designed to sit on a table.*

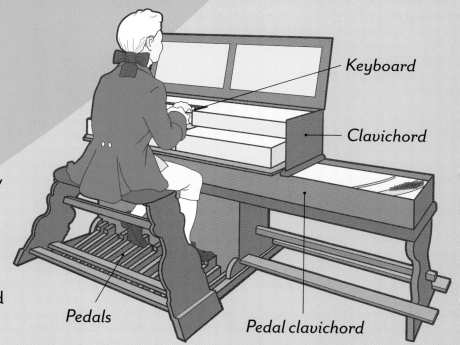

Keyboard

Clavichord

Pedals

Pedal clavichord

## Striking a note

Clavichords are typically small and compact and they can be placed on a table for playing. When a player presses a key, a small metal blade, called a tangent, strikes a pair of metal strings and causes them to vibrate and make a sound. The player cannot make the sounds louder or softer by pressing the keys of a clavichord harder or more gently.

## Pedal power

Sometimes, a second clavichord was placed underneath the first one. It was called a pedal clavichord and was worked by pedals with the feet. The pedal clavichord played lower notes. Organists often used them to practise on because the only organs were in churches and were not always available.

# Hurdy gurdy

The hurdy gurdy is an unusual instrument with a lively sound. It has strings, like a violin, but it also has a keyboard. In Europe, it is often used to play folk music and accompany folk dancing. It is also called a wheel fiddle.

## Hurdy gurdy design

The most common type of hurdy gurdy has a wooden, violin-shaped, body with six strings. Traditionally, the strings are made from animal gut but today, they are usually made from metal.

*Today, hurdy gurdies are often played at folk festivals and celebrations.*

## Wheels and strings

To play a hurdy gurdy, a player uses one hand to turn the crank at one end and the other to play the keyboard. Turning the crank makes a wheel spin round and rub against the strings. This causes them to vibrate. Pressing the keys of the hurdy gurdy makes tangents (small wooden wedges) press against the strings, changing the pitch of the notes.

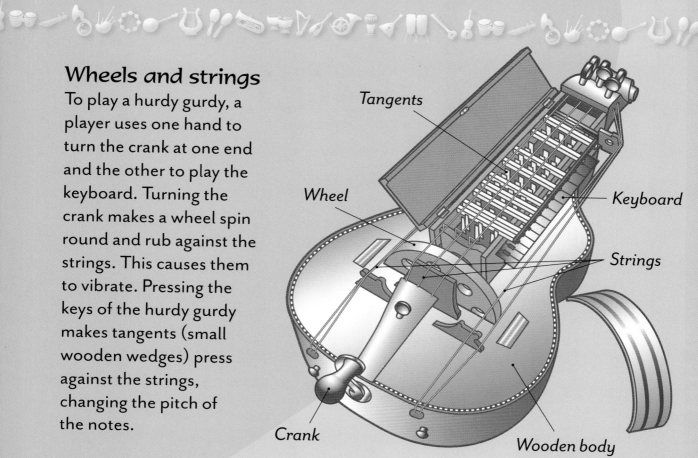

Tangents

Wheel

Keyboard

Strings

Crank

Wooden body

## Musical Notes

The organistrum was an early hurdy gurdy. It was so big that it had to be played by two people. One turned the crank and the other pulled the keys upwards. It was so tricky to play that it could only be used for playing slow tunes.

# Church organ

The organ is one of the oldest keyboard instruments and has been played for thousands of years. Organs can make a wide range of sounds, from low and quiet, to very loud and dramatic. They are most often used to play religious music in churches and synagogues.

*This is the organ console in the Royal Albert Hall, London, showing its four keyboards and many stops and pedals.*

## Parts of an organ

A large organ has a range of pipes of different sizes, varying in length from 2.5 centimetres to about 10 metres. The pipes produce different sounds and can be open or stopped. Stopped pipes produce lower sounds. There are also three to four keyboards, a pedal board and a range of knobs, called stops.

*The largest organs may have more than 15,000 pipes and as many as 2,000 stops.*

## Musical Notes

*The first organ was invented in ancient Greece in around 250 BCE. It used water power to blow air through the pipes. Modern organs use electric fans to produce an air supply.*

## Playing the organ

An organist sits at the console (the organ's control panel) and plays the organ with his hands and feet. To select a range of pipes, he pulls out some of the stops. When the player presses down on a key or pedal, air passes into the pipes and produces sounds. Each keyboard works a different set of pipes.

# Accordion

Also known as a squeezebox, the accordion is a box-shaped instrument that has been played since the early 19th century. Its wheezy sound is popular in folk music, especially in Europe and in North and South America.

## Accordion design

An accordion is two wooden boxes, joined together by bellows. The bellows are made from pleated layers of cloth and cardboard . Inside the boxes are set of metal strips, called reeds. There are keyboards at either end of the accordion, with buttons or piano-style keys made from ivory or plastic. Each end has a metal grid to let air in and out, and project the sound.

Bellows

Wooden box

Wooden box

Keyboard

Keys

Metal grid

Buttons

Keyboard

## One-person band

A player straps the accordion to her front and plays it with both hands. She pulls or squeezes the bellows and presses the buttons and keys to let air flow over the reeds. This makes the reeds vibrate to produce sounds. A player usually plays the melody with her right hand and the accompaniment with her left.

## Musical Notes

*It is thought that the accordion was invented by German instrument-maker, Christian Friedrich Ludwig Buschmann (1805 – 1864). His father built organs and Friedrich helped him with his work.*

*A musician playing an accordion at a folk festival in Norway. She plays the melody on the piano-style keyboard and the accompaniment on the button keyboard.*

# Harmonium

The harmonium sounds similar to the accordion, and works in much the same way. Air is blown through sets of metal reeds to make sounds. The player plays the tune on a keyboard.

## Upright harmonium

Harmoniums from North America and Europe look like small organs, or upright pianos. The player sits at a stool and works a set of pedals with her feet to fill the bellows with air. She plays the melody and chords on the keyboard with both left and right hands. This type of harmonium is also called a reed organ.

## Musical Notes

*Harmoniums were very popular in Europe in the late 19th and early 20th centuries. They were used in small churches and chapels where there was not enough space for a large organ. They were also played in people's homes.*

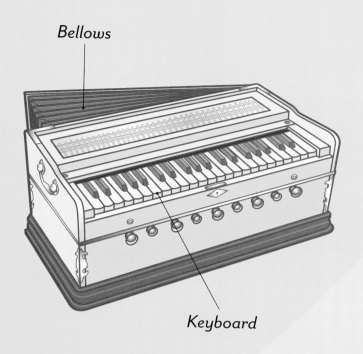

Bellows

Keyboard

## Indian harmonium

The harmonium was brought to India from Europe in the 19th century. The Indian harmonium is smaller and can easily be carried about. It is very popular in Indian classical, folk and religious music, and is used to play music for Indian films. The player sits on the floor and plays the melody with one hand, while working the bellows with the other.

*A group of street musicians playing the harmonium and other instruments in India.*

# Melodica

**M**elodicas are keyboard instruments, related to harmonicas, or mouth organs. They are mostly made from plastic or wood, and are small and light enough to be carried around. Melodicas are popular around the world, and can be heard on many rock and pop songs. They produce a quite thin, reedy sound, like an oboe.

## Melodica playing

A player holds the melodica in his hands and blows through a mouthpiece that fits into a hole at one end of the instrument. As he presses a key on the keyboard on top, a hole opens and allows air to flow across a reed inside to make a sound.

*A musician playing a melodica. Melodicas feature in many different types of music.*

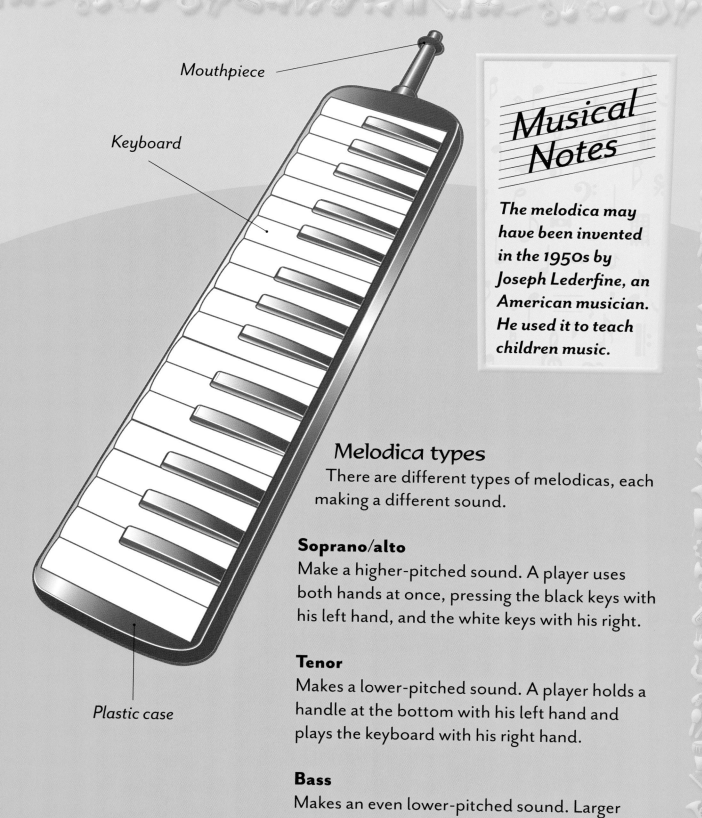

Mouthpiece

Keyboard

Plastic case

## Musical Notes

The melodica may have been invented in the 1950s by Joseph Lederfine, an American musician. He used it to teach children music.

## Melodica types

There are different types of melodicas, each making a different sound.

**Soprano/alto**

Make a higher-pitched sound. A player uses both hands at once, pressing the black keys with his left hand, and the white keys with his right.

**Tenor**

Makes a lower-pitched sound. A player holds a handle at the bottom with his left hand and plays the keyboard with his right hand.

**Bass**

Makes an even lower-pitched sound. Larger reeds produce an accordion-like sound.

# Carillon

For centuries, bells have been rung from churches in Europe and around the world. A carillon is a musical instrument, made from set of 20 or more bronze bells and often hung in a bell tower or church belfry.

## Carillon chords

Each bell is made to ring by a rope attached to the clapper inside, or by a hammer on the outside. The simplest type of carillon is played by pulling on the ropes. More complicated carillons are played with a keyboard. The player hits the keys with his fists and presses pedals with his feet. The keys activate levers that pull the ropes or work the hammers.

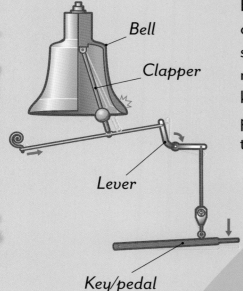

Bell

Clapper

Lever

Key/pedal

*This is the keyboard of a carillon in the tower of St Nicholas Kirk in Scotland. It has 48 bells.*

# Celeste

The celeste looks like an piano but it is actually a type of glockenspiel. An ordinary glockenspiel has two rows of metal bars that are played with hard beaters to give a strong, bell-like sound. A celeste is a glockenspiel with a keyboard. The keys are connected to felt-covered hammers that strike the metal bars.

*From the outside, this celeste looks just like an ordinary piano but it works like a glockenspiel.*

## Musical Notes

A glockenspiel is a percussion instrument similar to a xylophone, but it has bars made of metal instead of wood.

## Celestial music

In French, 'celeste' means 'heavenly', and describes the instrument's soft tone. The celeste is played in classical music, jazz and film scores to give a dream-like sound. It features in the Dance of the Sugarplum Fairy from Tchaikovsky's ballet The Nutcracker.

# Electronic keyboard

Today, electronic instruments are widely played, especially in pop and rock music. The most popular electronic instrument is the electronic keyboard. Some electronic keyboards stand alone and have their own speakers. Others are connected to a separate amplifier and speaker.

*This electronic keyboard has 76 keys. It can easily be carried from place to place to be played.*

## Convenient keyboards

Electronic keyboards come in a range of sizes, and are often small enough to be carried about in a case. Electronic pianos are larger and have the same number of keys as an ordinary piano. Electronic keyboards can be used for playing many different types of music and, unlike ordinary keyboards, never need tuning. Many can produce the sounds of many different musical instruments.

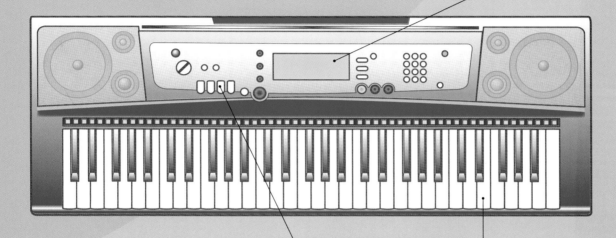

*Display screen*

*Sound and rhythm selector*

*Keyboard*

## Musical Notes

**The Rocksichord is an electronic keyboard invented in the 1960s. It was designed to sound like a harpsichord and was used in rock and jazz music.**

## Learning to play

Electronic keyboards are often used to teach children how to play. Keyboards can be connected to computers so that learners can use teaching software, and can also record their playing. There are differences between playing an electric keyboard and a piano. When you press down a piano key, the note plays, then gradually dies away. On an electronic keyboard, the note stays the same as long as the key is pressed.

# Synthesizer

A synthesizer is an electronic instrument that is played like a piano or organ. But it is more than simply an electronic keyboard. By using the controls above the keys, a player can produce a huge variety of sounds and mix them together to make a piece of music. The sounds can be of traditional instruments or new and unusual sounds.

*Since the 1960s, synthesizers like this have become very important instruments in many different type of music, particularly rock and pop.*

## How a synthesizer works

A synthesizer produces electrical signals which are then amplified and sent to speakers or headphones. The keyboard is used to start and stop the sounds. Various knobs and other controls change the sounds.

*Synthesizers can look like pianos, or guitars. Here, legendary musician Stevie Wonder plays a guitar synthesizer at the Glastonbury Festival.*

## Musical Notes

*Modern synthesizers are digital. This means that the sounds are represented by numbers inside electronic circuits.*

## Rock revolution

Synthesizers became very popular in the late 1960s, with the invention of the Moog synthesizer. Many rock and pop musicians began to use synthesizers on their albums and in their live concerts. In the 1980s and 90s, they became one of the most important instruments in pop and were used by bands such as Kraftwerk, Ultravox and Depeche Mode.

# Words to remember

**amplifier**
An electric device that increases the volume of an instrument.

**bass**
The lower notes in music.

**belfry**
The part of a church tower in which the bells are hung.

**bellows**
Part of an instrument made from pleated cloth or cardboard that is used to produce a flow of air.

**chamber music**
Music performed by a small group of musicians, originally in a chamber, or room.

**cylinder**
A long, tube-like object.

**ebony**
A very hard, tropical wood that was once used to make the black keys on a piano keyboard.

**horizontally**
Lying level or flat.

**ivory**
The material that an elephant's tusks are made from that was once used to make the white keys on a piano keyboard.

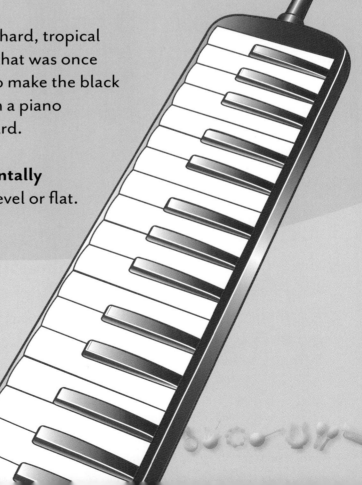

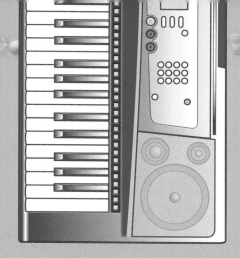

**keyboard**
A set of keys, usually worked by being pressed or touched by hand.

**key**
A part of a musical instrument that is pressed or touched to make a sound.

**oboe**
A type of wind instrument that makes a thin, reedy sound.

**plectrum**
A piece of quill, plastic or wood that is used to pluck a string.

**quill**
A hard material made from the long, hollow part of a bird's feather.

**reed**
A thin strip of metal or cane inside a musical instrument.

**synagogue**
A place where Jewish people go to meet and worship.

**treble**
The higher notes in music.

**vertically**
Standing upright.

**vibrate**
To move to and fro

# Index

accordian 5, 18-19
aerophones 5

carillon 5, 24
celeste 5, 25
chordophones 5
clavichord 5, 12-13
Cristofori, Bartolomeu 7

electronic keyboard 26
electrophones 5

glockenspiel 25
grand piano 8

Handel, Georg
  Friedrich 12
harmonica 22
harmonium 5, 20
harpsichord 5, 10
hurdy gurdy 5, 14-15

idiophones 5
Indian harmonium 21

keyboard 5
keys 5, 6

melodica 5, 22-23
Moog synthesizer 5, 29

organ 5, 16-17
organistrum 15

pedal clavichord 13
piano 5, 6-7
pianola 7
plectrum 11, 31

Rocksichord 27

synthesizer 5, 28-29

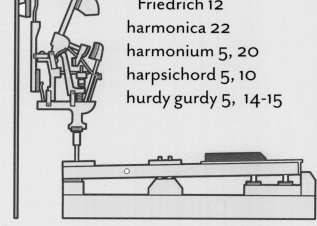